‹HAITI›

MAJOR WORLD NATIONS

HAITI

Suzanne Anthony

CHELSEA HOUSE PUBLISHERS
Philadelphia

Chelsea House Publishers

Contributing Author: Derek Davis

Copyright © 1999 by Chelsea House Publishers,
a subsidiary of Haights Cross Communications.
All rights reserved.
Printed and bound in Malaysia.

3   5   7   9   8   6   4

Library of Congress Cataloging-in-Publication Data

Anthony, Suzanne.
Haiti.

Includes index.
Summary: Surveys the history, topography, people, and culture of
Haiti, with emphasis on its current economy, industry, and place
in the political world.
1. Haiti—Juvenile Literature. [1. Haiti]
I. Title.
F1915.2.A58   1988   972.94   87-18251
ISBN 0-7910-4759-8

◄CONTENTS►

Map 6

Facts at a Glance 9

History at a Glance 11

Chapter 1 Haiti and the World 17

Chapter 2 Land of Mountains 27

Chapter 3 A Prosperous Colony 39

Chapter 4 Revolt and Independence 49

Color Section Scenes of Haiti 57

Chapter 5 Government and Economy 77

Chapter 6 People and Ways of Life 85

Chapter 7 Cultural Life 95

Chapter 8 Haiti in Review 103

Glossary 105

Index 107

CUBA

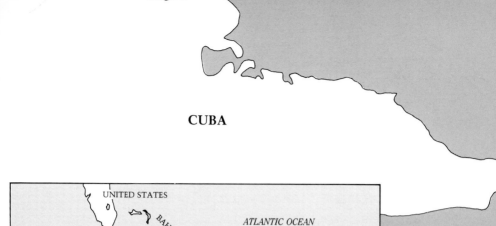

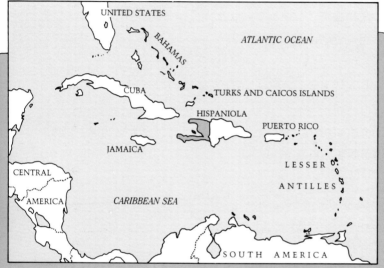

UNITED STATES

ATLANTIC OCEAN

BAHAMAS

CUBA

TURKS AND CAICOS ISLANDS

HISPANIOLA

PUERTO RICO

JAMAICA

LESSER

ANTILLES

CENTRAL

CARIBBEAN SEA

AMERICA

SOUTH AMERICA

WINDWARD

Jérémie

JAMAICA

CARIBBEAN SEA

PASSAGE

TORTUGA

Port-de-Paix •

Cap-Haïtien
La Navidad

• Môle St. Nicolas

MASSIF DU   NORD

Vertières

Fort Liberté

▲ Sans Souci Palace

▲ Citadelle La Ferrìere

Trois   *Rivières*

• Gonaïves

GULF OF
GONÂVE

MONTAGNES NOIRES

• Hinche

HAITI

Artibonite R.

L. PÉLIGRE

Péligre Dam

DOMINICAN

REPUBLIC

ST. MARC CHANNEL

LA GONÂVE

Ville Bonheur • ▲

Saut d'Eau

L. SAUMÂTRE

GONÂVE
CHANNEL

GRANDE CAYEMITE

Port-au-Prince

• Pétionville

Grande   Anse R.   *L. MIRAGOÂNE*

MASSIF DU SUD

MORNE DE LA SELLE ▲

MASSIF DE LA SELLE

Jacmel •

• Les Cayes

ÎLE À VACHE

◄ FACTS AT A GLANCE ►

Land and People

Area	10,714 square miles (27,750 square kilometers)
National Name	République d'Haïti
Capital	Port-au-Prince
Other Cities	Cap-Haïtien, Pétionville, Gonaïves, Les Cayes
Highest Point	Pic la Selle, 8,793 feet (2,674 meters)
Major Mountains	Massif du Nord, Massif du Sud, Massif de la Selle, Montagnes Noires
Major Rivers	Artibonite, Trois Riviéres, Grande Anse
Major Lakes	Saumâtre, Péligre, Miragoâne
Major Islands	La Gonâve, Tortuga, Grande Cayemite, Île à Vache
Population	7 million
Population Density	650 people per sq. mile (240 per sq. km)
Population Distribution	Rural, 70 percent; urban, 30 percent
Official Languages	French, Creole
Ethnic Groups	Black, 95 percent; mulatto (mixed black and white), 5 percent
Religions	Roman Catholic, 80 percent; Baptist, 10 percent; other (mostly Protestant), 10 percent; in addition, nearly all Haitians are Voodooists (followers of African-based Voodoo religion)
Literacy Rate	35 to 40 percent
Life Expectancy	Men, 47 years; women, 51 years
Infant Mortality	104/1,000 live births

Government

Form of Government   Constitutional republic with legislative body

Legislative Body   National Assembly: Senate, 27 members; Chamber of Deputies, 83 members

Official Head of State and Government   President

Local Government   Nine *départements* (provinces), divided into *communes* (counties) and *bourgs* (townships); also several rural districts

Constitution   Approved by voters, 1987

Voting Rights   All men and women over age 18

Economy

Currency   Gourde, divided into 100 centimes; approximately 15–20 gourdes equal U.S. $1

Average Annual Income $340, lowest in Western Hemisphere

Land Use   Farming, 33 percent; pastures, 18 percent; forests, 4 percent; other (including eroded farmland or wasteland), 45 percent

Gross Domestic Product $6 billion

Percentage of GDP   Agriculture, 35 percent; manufacturing, 23 percent; services, 42 percent

Major Agricultural Products   Coffee, sugarcane, bananas, sisal, mangoes, corn, rice

Major Industrial Products   Cement, toys, electronic equipment, cotton cloth

◄HISTORY AT A GLANCE►

about 2000 B.C.	Indians known as the Ciboney migrate to the West Indies from Central or South America. Some of them settle in present-day Haiti.
300 B.C. to 100 A.D.	New tribes, called the Arawak, arrive from South America. Those who settle in Haiti are called the Taino. They introduce agriculture and pottery. The Taino kill or intermarry with the Ciboney, except for a few Ciboney who retreat into southwestern Haiti.
1492	Columbus sights the island of Hispaniola during his first voyage to the New World. His flagship is wrecked on a reef off the northern coast. Columbus returns to Spain in a different ship, leaving 39 men in La Navidad, the first European colony in the Americas.
1493	Columbus returns to La Navidad and finds that his men have been killed. He establishes a new colony in the present-day Dominican Republic.
1498	Columbus sets up headquarters at the site of present-day Santo Domingo. He governs Hispaniola until 1500.
1500s	Spain governs Hispaniola as an agricultural colony. Most of the Indians are killed or die of disease. Early in the century, black slaves are brought from Africa to work on the plantations (mostly sugarcane).
early 1600s	French pirates begin to settle in Tortuga and western Hispaniola.

1664   The French West India Company founds the city of Port-de-Paix on the northwest coast.

1670   Cap-Français is founded on the site of present-day Cap-Haïtien.

1697   The Treaty of Ryswick gives the western third of Hispaniola to the French, who name it Saint-Domingue.

1700s   Saint-Domingue becomes the most prosperous colony in the New World and France's proudest possession. Thousands of slaves are brought to the island, and millions of tons of sugar are shipped to France.

1760   The white colonists begin to make laws that limit the rights of the free mulattoes.

1789   On the eve of the French Revolution, Saint-Domingue has about 500,000 slaves, 32,000 whites, and 24,000 mulattoes. Two-thirds of France's overseas investments are in Saint-Domingue.

1791   The Revolution in France brings unrest to the colony. Rioting breaks out. Slave revolts in the north spread to the rest of the colony. Many whites are massacred; others flee the island.

1794   Slavery is officially abolished, but the colony remains in a state of armed revolt.

1795   Spain gives the eastern two-thirds of the island to France. The Spanish portion is quickly taken over by the former slaves, led by Toussaint L'Ouverture, who rules the entire island.

1801 to 1802   Toussaint L'Ouverture names himself governor-general of Saint-Domingue. He plans to turn the colony back over to French rule but is sent to prison in France.

1803   Jean-Jacques Dessalines and Henri Christophe

lead black armies to victory against the invading French.

1804   Hispaniola is declared independent under the Arawak name Haiti, the second republic in the Western Hemisphere. Dessalines adopts the title Emperor Jacques I.

1806   Dessalines is killed. Christophe takes control of Haiti.

1808   Britain helps Spain regain control of the eastern part of the island. Haiti is reduced to its present-day boundaries.

1808 to 1820   Civil war divides the country between Christophe in the north and Alexandre Sabès Pétion and Jean-Pierre Boyer in the south. Christophe commits suicide in 1820.

1818   Pétion dies. Boyer becomes president of all of southern Haiti.

1820   Upon Christophe's death, Boyer becomes president of the entire nation.

1822   Boyer invades and conquers Santo Domingo, the Spanish portion of the island.

1843   Boyer's rule is overthrown.

1844   The Santo Domingans drive out the Haitians and declare their area the Dominican Republic.

1843 to 1915   Haiti is governed by 22 rulers, mostly dictators placed in power by the army. Revolutions or political assassinations end the careers of most of them.

1915   Vilbrun Guillaume Sam seizes the presidency with the help of mercenaries. After he is killed by a mob, the U.S. Marines invade Haiti to restore order and protect American business and political interests.

1915 to 1934	Haiti is governed by a U.S. occupying force.
1930	Haitians elect Sténio Vincent president in an election supervised by the Americans. Vincent remains in power until 1941.
1934	American military forces withdraw from Haiti.
1937	The Dominican Republic protests that Haitians are entering the Republic illegally. Dominican militiamen kill thousands of Haitians along the border.
1946	The army makes Dumarsais Estimé president.
1947	The U.S. gives up its control of Haiti's treasury and finances.
1950 to 1956	General Paul Magloire is president.
1957	François Duvalier, called "Papa Doc," is elected president.
1964	Duvalier abolishes Haiti's constitution and declares himself president for life. He rules the country as a police state with himself as the sole source of power.
1966	Pope Paul VI excommunicates Duvalier from the Roman Catholic church.
1971	Duvalier dies. His son Jean-Claude Duvalier, called "Baby Doc," succeeds him as president for life. At age 19, Duvalier is the world's youngest president.
1980	Duvalier marries Michèle Bennett. The people's outrage at the lavish wedding and the Duvaliers' repressive rule leads to protests, riots, and police crackdowns.
1986	A violent uprising forces the Duvaliers to flee to France. The National Council of Government (CNG), a committee of army officers, takes control of the country.

1987   Haitians adopt a new constitution, their 23rd since independence.

1988   Leslie Manigat, a former professor, is elected president but is unseated six months later in a military coup. Haiti undergoes four more changes of regime, most by army coup, by 1990.

1990   Jesuit priest and populist Jean-Bertrand Aristide is elected president and attempts to institute reforms.

1991   Aristide is overthrown by military coup and goes into exile in the United States.

1994   Following United Nations sanctions against the military regime and the threat of U.N. invasion, Aristide is allowed to return and finish out his term as president.

1995   René Préval, Aristide's first prime minister, is elected to succeed Aristide as president.

Among Haiti's most critical problems are the shortage of adequate housing and the loss of most of the nation's woodlands and its fertile topsoil.

Haiti and
the World

Haiti, an independent republic in the West Indies, occupies one-third of
the mountainous tropical island of Hispaniola. Bordered on the north
by the Atlantic Ocean and on the south and east by the Caribbean Sea,
Haiti shares its eastern border with the Dominican Republic, which occupies the eastern two-thirds of the island. Haiti's next closest neighbors are Cuba, 57 miles (90 kilometers) to the northwest, and Jamaica,
about 116 miles (180 km) to the southwest. Haiti is some 565 miles
(900 km) southeast of Florida.

About 95 percent of Haiti's more than 7 million residents are
black, the descendants of Africans brought to the New World as slaves
between the 16th and 18th centuries. The remainder of Haiti's people are
predominantly *mulattoes* (of mixed black and white ancestry). Haiti is the
only nation ever created by a slave revolt. It was the world's first black republic and the second New World colony (after the United States) to gain
independence.

Haiti is a land of stark contrasts. Some of its scenery is breath-
taking: Snowy clouds and brilliant blue sky surmount rugged limestone peaks; swift rivers race to the sea across white sandy beaches
adorned by palm trees. Offsetting this natural beauty, however, are
scenes of desolation: Most of Haiti's once dense woodlands have been

A slum area called "Tokyo" in Port-au-Prince reflects Haiti's poverty and overcrowding.

stripped, their topsoil washed away, their desertlike acres now supporting only thorns and cactus.

At one time the richest colony in the Americas, Haiti is now the poorest nation in the Western Hemisphere. It is, in fact, among the most impoverished—and densely populated—countries in the world. The majority of its people are farmers who struggle for survival on tiny, unproductive plots of land. Although a handful of plantation owners raise sugarcane, cotton, bananas, and coffee beans for export, most of Haiti's farming families grow little more than they consume themselves.

Haiti has no rich mineral resources. Its few assembly factories, which produced baseballs, toys, and electronic goods for export, closed due to the economic sanctions imposed by the United Nations during the illegal military regime of the early 1990s. They have been slow in recovering and providing employment. Items such as cars, medicines, electrical goods, and petroleum must be imported. Like other developing nations emerging from agricultural ways into the modern industrial age, Haiti lags far behind such great industrial powers as the United States, Germany, and Japan in income, health, education, and general standards of living. Most of the developing nations are in Africa, Latin America, and southern Asia. Many are new, created within the past century from colonies once ruled by European powers. And many are faced with serious economic, social, and political problems.

Haiti's fortunes have undergone an astonishing transformation since the 18th century. Throughout the 1700s, it was a French colony known as Saint-Domingue. Nicknamed the Grand Isle à Sucre (the Great Sugar Island), Saint-Domingue accounted for two-thirds of France's foreign trade. Frenchmen who settled here prospered mightily: "Rich as a Dominguan" became a common phrase. The colony's immense wealth was based on Europeans' insatiable appetite for sugar; each year, the French colony's huge plantations produced thousands of tons of sugarcane, which was refined into millions of pounds of sugar and shipped across the Atlantic.

The cane grew well in Saint-Domingue's tropical climate, but clearing the land and harvesting the crop was backbreaking work. To meet their labor needs, French landowners brought shipload after shipload of slaves from West Africa to Saint-Domingue. Soon the black slaves vastly outnumbered their white owners. By 1789, Haiti's population consisted of some 32,000 whites and 500,000 slaves. Be-

In the 1700s, slaves and sugarcane made the white colonists fabulously rich.

tween these groups were 24,000 *gens de couleur* (literally, "people of color"), mulattoes born to free white fathers and black slave mothers.

Few slaves were treated humanely in the New World, but those brought to Saint-Domingue were subjected to almost unimaginable cruelty. Vastly outnumbered by their slaves, French slave owners lived in constant fear of a black revolt. To maintain control, they enforced iron discipline, inflicting savage punishments on their slaves for the slightest offense. One historian called Saint-Domingue "a mill for crushing Negroes as much for crushing sugar cane." Under such brutal conditions, a massive slave uprising was almost inevitable, and in 1791, it began. In 1804, after years of warfare that pitted blacks against whites, Haitians against the armies of France and Spain, Haiti became a republic, free of both slavery and French rule.

The Haitian people were and continue to be tremendously proud of their triumphant fight for independence. But although the revolt freed them from slavery, it left them chained to poverty. The liberated Haitians, no longer forced to work on lands owned by others, carved out their own small farms and began to raise corn, vegetables, and fruits to feed their families. The great plantations, however, had been destroyed—and the huge cash income produced by sugar was gone with them. After independence, very few Haitians possessed even a fraction of the wealth enjoyed by their former masters.

Along with economic hardship, freedom brought political troubles. Haiti's citizens had no experience in self-government, and they were spread out over a country that offered only primitive means of travel and communication. Power-hungry men found it easy to seize control of the new nation and set themselves up as rulers. In the years since independence, Haiti's history has been studded with frequent assassinations, military takeovers, and dictatorships. Conflicts with the Dominican Republic, the former Spanish colony that oc-

After more than 200 years of brutal oppression, the black slaves of Saint-Domingue rebelled against the French landowners and the army of Napoléon Bonaparte.

cupies the eastern two-thirds of Hispaniola, have also played a large part in the country's turbulent development.

To prevent invasion by other nations, United States troops occupied Haiti in 1915 and remained for nearly two decades. Once they left, political instability returned. In 1986, Haitians drove out dictator Jean-Claude Duvalier; he and his father had ruled for 29 years. A new constitution (1987) offered hope for a democratic government, but a series of military coups intervened. In 1990, populist priest Jean-Bertrand Aristide was elected president, but the military exiled him until the United Nations threatened invasion. Though Aristide returned, the U.N. kept troops in Haiti to assure stability and retrain the police, which the Duvaliers and their military successors had used to control the population through fear.

Along with political chaos, Haiti is plagued by food shortages, severe public-health problems, and a disastrous decline in the economically crucial tourist industry. The food crisis results directly from the loss of Haiti's formerly lush forests. Nearly all the nation's trees have been felled for fuel or to clear land for farms; efforts to replant them have so far proved unsuccessful. Without its forest cover, Haiti has lost most of the precious topsoil that once made its acres fertile and productive. Large parts of the country are nothing but bare limestone or thin, dry, exhausted soil in which no crops will grow.

Some of the few still-fertile areas have been returned to sugarcane cultivation, producing a crop that Haiti can sell to other countries for cash. The remaining farmland is not sufficient to raise enough food for Haiti's people. The country is forced to spend much of its limited income to import food. Even with the costly food

Today, much of Haiti has been reduced to barren, unproductive wasteland.

imports, however, malnutrition takes thousands of lives, mostly among infants and young children, each year.

Nationwide health programs, many of them supported by foreign aid, have wiped out some of the diseases that once stalked Haiti, but malaria, tuberculosis, and dysentery remain as killers. And in the early 1980s, a new medical crisis brought Haiti to the world's attention: the deadly disease AIDS (acquired immune deficiency syndrome), first thought to have developed in Haiti, then later traced to central Africa. Following the 1994 return of President Aristide from exile, an infusion of aid and volunteer workers from members of the United Nations, especially the United States, began to attack the worst of Haiti's remaining health problems.

Haiti's AIDS epidemic crippled the profitable tourist industry, and continuing political instability only worsened the situation. In the 1950s, Haiti discovered that its tropical climate and beaches could attract thousands of tourists. The money spent by these well-to-do visitors became vitally important to Haiti's economy, helping to make up for the nation's lack of other resources. Although tourism lagged under the regime of François Duvalier, it revived after his son, Jean-Claude, took over the government in 1971.

In 1981, tourism brought Haiti U.S. $85 million, a sum that included real-estate investments by foreign corporations, wages paid to hotel and restaurant workers, and money spent by tourists on meals, crafts, and souvenirs. Government planners expected this sum to increase substantially in the years ahead. But political turmoil has kept foreign visitors away from Haiti, and the tourism industry has collapsed.

For all its past and present troubles, Haiti is a complex and fascinating land. It is a treasure house of history: Scholars believe that the remains of Christopher Columbus's wrecked flagship, the *Santa María*, lie offshore; the ruins of La Navidad, the first European settlement in the New World, were rediscovered on Haiti's north

The fortress built in the early 1800s by a former slave is now a national monument.

coast in the late 1980s; and the Citadel, a mighty early-19th-century fortress built by a slave who became a king, continues to dominate the sky from a northern mountaintop.

Haiti's unique culture is a blend of French and Roman Catholic traditions brought by early settlers and black African customs brought by the slaves. Haitians have mixed these strains to create their own language, called Creole, and their own religion, called Voodoo. Most recently, the spirit of Haiti's culture has materialized in an outpouring of paintings by untrained but often highly gifted artists. The colorful, lively, sometimes mystical works of the "Haitian school" of painters are finding favor among collectors and museums around the world.

In the centuries since Columbus's 1492 "discovery" of Hispaniola, Haiti has meant many things to the world. As a French colony, it represented sugar and great wealth. As a black republic founded by rebellious slaves, it became a sign of hope for oppressed peoples everywhere. Today, Haiti is a developing nation struggling against poverty, disease, and a legacy of poor leadership. Whether the coming years will bring further unrest or an upturn in Haiti's fortunes remains to be seen. But Haitians are a creative, patient, proud, and resourceful people; refusing to despair, many of them are determined to create a better life for themselves and their country.

Haiti is a land of rolling hills and rugged peaks, with valleys folded between them. In the desperate search for farmland, even steep hillsides are tilled.

Land of Mountains

To the Arawak Indians, who lived in the Caribbean area long before the arrival of Europeans, *haiti* meant "land of mountains." The word makes a fitting name for a nation whose landscape is dominated by steep, rugged peaks. Haiti occupies the western third of mountainous Hispaniola, the second largest island (after Cuba) in the Caribbean Sea. Sharing the island is the Dominican Republic, which is separated from its smaller neighbor by a 193-mile (311-km) border.

Cuba lies 57 miles (90 km) northwest of Haiti. Between the two countries is a strait, or channel, called the Windward Passage. This waterway, which links the Caribbean Sea to the Atlantic Ocean, has been vitally important as both a trade and a military route since Europeans sailed into the Caribbean in 1492.

About the same size as the U.S. state of Maryland, Haiti covers an area of 10,714 square miles (27,750 sq. km). In shape, the country resembles the claw of a giant crab with its pincers open. The pincers are two peninsulas, one in the north and one in the south, that run westward, away from the border with the Dominican Republic. Between the peninsulas lies the Gulf of Gonâve; in the middle of the gulf, like a tidbit about to be seized by the crab, is the island of La Gonâve.

The 850-mile (1,369-kilometer) coastline is dotted with hundreds of small fishing villages.

Only one-fifth of Haiti's territory can be considered lowland—that is, lower in altitude than about 600 feet (180 meters) above sea level. Of the remaining four-fifths of the country, about half consists of hills ranging from 600 to 1,500 feet (180 to 450 m) in height. The other half of the highlands—a total of 40 percent of the country—is studded with mountains higher than 1,500 feet (450 m). Nearly 60 percent of the country is too mountainous to be farmed.

The chief highland regions are the Massif du Nord, a mountain chain that runs across the northern peninsula and into the Dominican Republic; the Montagnes Noires and the Chaîne de Matheux, in the center of the country; the Massif du Sud, in the southern peninsula; and the Massif de la Selle, an easterly continuation of the Massif du Sud. The southern mountains are generally higher than those in the north. At 8,793 feet (2,674 m), the country's highest point is Pic la Selle in the southeast.

Instead of a flat expanse dotted with mountain ranges, Haiti is best pictured as a mass of hills and mountains separated by a few level areas, or lowlands. (An early European explorer reportedly described the island to his monarch by crumpling a map with both hands. "Your majesty," he said, "this is Hispaniola.") In Haiti's lowlands are the nation's main agricultural centers as well as its largest population centers.

Of the four principal lowland areas, the most important is the 150-square mile (390-sq. km) Plaine du Nord, near the city of Cap-Haïtien; this area contains the nation's richest soil and was the center of the old French colony. Another major lowland area, lying between the Massif du Nord and the Montagnes Noires, is the high Plaine Centrale. A grasslands region, it is used mainly for cattle-grazing. The Plaine de l'Artibonite, lying between the Montagnes Noires and the Chaîne de Matheux, is bordered by the Gulf of Gonâve and contains large areas of swampy land. The Cul-de-Sac, the smallest lowland, runs eastward from the capital city of Port-au-Prince into the Dominican Republic.

The mountain ranges and the lowlands of Haiti generally run west to east. This geographical pattern makes movement within the nation difficult; travel between north and south involves crossing the knife-edged ridges and steep slopes of the mountains. Increasing the difficulty of travel and communication within Haiti is the scarcity of telephones and automobiles, both of which are far too costly for the average citizen. As a result, many Haitians have little contact with people in other parts of the country or with national affairs.

Along Haiti's 850-mile (1,369-km) coastline are hundreds of bays, coves, and small sheltered harbors. Waters around the island are generally shallow, ranging from 4 to 10 feet (1 to 3 m) in depth, but several ports are suitable for deep-water ships. The smaller harbors are the sites of tiny fishing villages whose residents use handmade canoes and boats to fish the nearby waters. Some of these villages can be reached only by sea.

Haiti's territory includes a number of islands. The largest is La Gonâve, which is about 35 miles (56 km) long and 10 miles (16 km)

In the harbor of Port-au-Prince, boys dive for coins tossed from a ship.

wide. The island, which lies in the Gulf of Gonâve, off Port-au-Prince, is hilly and rugged. Although it receives little rainfall, local farmers raise small quantities of cotton and corn. La Gonâve is not extensively developed, but its excellent beaches and campgrounds make it a popular spot with the few Haitians who can afford to take vacations.

The second largest of Haiti's islands is Tortuga, also known as La Tortue. About 23 miles (37 km) long and 4 to 5 miles (6 to 8 km) wide, Tortuga lies off the northern coast, near the harbor of Port-de-Paix. During the 1600s, it was best known as a pirate stronghold; the seagoing bandits of the Caribbean often landed there to replenish their supplies with *tortugas* (Spanish for "tortoises") after which the island was named. Tortuga has no roads, but it boasts beautiful, unspoiled beaches swept by cool breezes. Developers had hoped to turn the island into a multimillion-dollar resort, but their plans were halted by the tourist industry's decline.

Two other sizable islands are Grande Cayemite, off the north coast of the southern peninsula, and Île à Vache (Cow Island) off the south coast. Both are densely populated. Haiti's shores are also rimmed with hundreds of tiny islets, some of them no more than spits of sand, but most of them inhabited. One such islet, called Lambi Island, is near Grande Cayemite. More than 200 Haitians live on this sandbar, which has no soil and no fresh water. Residents support themselves by fishing, and use their canoes to haul vegetables and water from the mainland five miles (eight km) away.

More than 100 rivers and streams flow from Haiti's highlands to the sea. Most are small, and many shrink or disappear entirely in very dry weather. Narrow, swift-flowing, and punctuated by waterfalls near their sources, these watercourses grow wider and slower as they approach the coasts. None are navigable, but many are used for irrigation. The larger and faster rivers are also potential sources of hydroelectric power for some of Haiti's most remote districts.

Haiti's longest river is the Artibonite, which rises in the Massif du Nord and flows through the broad Artibonite Plain for 174 miles (280 km) before emptying into the Gulf of Gonâve. In the north is the Trois Rivières, which reaches the sea near the coastal town of

Residents of the offshore islets haul vegetables and water from the mainland.

Port-de-Paix. The Grande Anse drains much of the southern peninsula, and the Massacre and Pedernales rivers form part of Haiti's border with the Dominican Republic.

Near the Dominican border, east of Port-au-Prince, is Étang Saumâtre, Haiti's largest lake, which covers 70 square miles (182 sq. km). Because Saumâtre's water is brackish (slightly salty), it is unsuitable for irrigation purposes. But it is suitable, according to some sources, for alligators up to 4.5 meters (almost 15 feet) long, many of which are said to inhabit the lake's cloudy waters. The nearby and much smaller Lake Miragoâne is also brackish. To the north, however, is Lake Péligre, a 10-mile (16 km) body of fresh water created when a large dam was built on the Artibonite River in the mid-1950s. The Péligre Dam, which now provides irrigation water for much of the Artibonite Plain, is the site of Haiti's first hydroelectric plant, completed in 1971.

Climate and Weather

Haiti lies between the Tropic of Cancer and the equator, which puts it in the earth's north tropical zone. It is not as hot as most tropical lands, however, because temperatures grow cooler as altitude increases, and most of Haiti is well above sea level. In addition, the low-lying coastal areas are cooled by steady sea breezes.

Because it is a tropical country, Haiti does not experience the sharp temperature changes that mark the seasons in nontropical lands. The average temperature in January and February is 75 degrees Fahrenheit (24 degrees centigrade), only a little cooler than the average July and August temperature of 83 degrees F (28 degrees C). Port-au-Prince, the capital, has an average annual temperature of 80 degrees F (27 degrees C), accompanied by high humidity during the summer months.

Rainfall varies by season and by location. Most of the rain that falls on the island of Hispaniola is carried by moist north and east winds that blow across the Dominican Republic before reaching Haiti. The higher mountains in the eastern half of the island trap much of the rain, making the Dominican Republic considerably wetter than Haiti. In Haiti, the highlands generally receive more rain than the lowlands. The northeastern mountains are the wettest part of the country, with about 100 inches (2,540 millimeters) of rain each year. The tips of the two peninsulas are the driest parts, receiving average annual rainfalls of only 20 inches (508 mm).

Small as it is, Haiti has two distinct patterns of wet and dry seasons. In the north, most of the rain falls from November through March. In the south, however, more rain falls from April through October. Port-au-Prince actually has two wet seasons; it receives nearly all of its rain from April through June and from August through November. Rain usually falls at night, when temperatures drop slightly; at all times of the year, the days are usually sunny.

Haiti lies in the "hurricane path" of the Caribbean. The hurricane season typically begins in August, reaches a peak in September and October, and ends in November. Hurricanes—powerful, slow-moving storms whose destructive forces include heavy rains, floods, cyclonic winds, and tidal waves—have wrought vast destruction in Haiti. In 1963, Hurricane Flora's torrential rains and shrieking winds

Destructive tropical storms often howl across the island on the Caribbean "hurricane path."

took thousands of lives and left a path of ruin. Another hurricane, this one named Allen, roared across the country in 1980, destroying houses, farms, and businesses, and weakening Haiti's already shaky economy.

Plant and Animal Life

When the first European settlers came to Hispaniola, the island was covered by dense forests. Such trees as mahogany, rosewood, cedar, and lignum vitae, all prized by the furniture makers of Europe, became one of the island's first profitable exports. Coconut palms and fruit trees flourished along the coasts and in the lowlands; the highlands were covered by a thick blanket of Caribbean pines, oaks, and other timber trees. Today, only a few scraps of that rich forest remain.

Over the years, nearly all of Haiti's trees have been destroyed. Farmers have cleared new plots with axes and machetes; where they found woodlands too steep for farming, they cut trees for lumber or fuel. By the late 1980s, only 6 wooded areas larger than 20 square miles (52 sq. km) remained in the country. The border between Haiti and the Dominican Republic offers grim evidence of a ravaged land: Haiti's side is brown and dry, but on the Dominican side, a thick carpet of lush green trees grows right down to the boundary line.

Many developing countries face deforestation problems, but Haiti's is especially serious. Without tree roots to anchor the soil, the mountainous terrain and fast-flowing streams allow topsoil to wash into the sea at a staggering rate. As tree cover decreases, the streams flow even faster, making the problem still worse. Reforestation programs have been replacing about 20 percent of the trees cut each year, but almost as soon as they are planted, these new trees are felled by people who need them for firewood or who hope to grow food crops on the land.

Deforestation is a vicious circle. It results from the need for more farms to feed a growing population, but in the long run, it makes the land less productive. Recently, the introduction of gourmet coffee trees has encouraged some local reforestation, but the island's increasing population may offset such efforts. The number of Haitians doubled between 1950 and 1985 and is expected to double again by the year 2015, though mass emigration to the United States following Aristide's overthrow delayed much of this projected increase.

Despite the wholesale destruction of its trees, Haiti still has a few patches of green. Most are in the remote mountain areas of the south, where small, isolated stands of pine and mahogany have escaped the woodsman's ax. Also growing in these remnants of Haiti's original forest are giant fern trees and wild orchids. A scattering of Caribbean pine trees remains in the Massif de la Selle in the southwest, and in the lowlands, farmers cultivate trees that bear mangoes, avocados, oranges, limes, and cherries.

Haiti's coasts are lined with mangrove swamps—dense clusters of low, twisted trees whose roots are covered by the sea at high tide. In some areas, where the original forest cover was cut down but where the land is too steep or too eroded for farming, a secondary growth of shrubs and scrubby thorn and guava trees has sprung up. In the drier sections of the Central Plateau, the Artibonite Plain, and the two peninsulas, nothing survives but cactus plants, thornbushes, and tough desert grasses.

Many of the nation's small farmers raise goats, pigs, or, less commonly, cows. All these animals were originally imported to Haiti, whose only native mammals are mice, moles, shrews, and other rodents. Also native to the country is an abundant supply of reptiles, fish, and birds.

Reptile life includes chameleons, three species of crocodile, many species of snake, and a lizard called (because of the fleshy spike on its nose) the rhino-horned iguana. Turtles, frogs, and salamanders also thrive in Haiti. The nation's rivers and coastal waters are

Haiti has no native livestock, but goats, pigs, and cows have been imported.

home to some 270 species of fish, of which the most important for food and sport fishing are the red snapper, tarpon, and kingfish. Hundreds of species of colorful reef fish—as well as barracuda—are found in the offshore reefs.

More than 200 species of birds have been sighted in Haiti. They include bright-colored tropical parrots, wild ducks, and many types of pigeon and pheasant. Graceful white egrets and pink flamingos nest by the thousands in the shallow, brackish waters of the Saumâtre and Miragoâne lakes. Haiti is also home to numerous insects, spiders, centipedes, and scorpions. Although many of them are poisonous, their bites are rarely fatal to humans. The most troublesome insect pest is the anopheles mosquito, which carries the parasitic organism that causes malaria, a serious tropical disease that afflicts many Haitians.

A statue of Christopher Columbus stands in Port-au-Prince. The explorer sighted the island on December 6, 1492, and named it La Isla Española (the Spanish Island).

A Prosperous Colony

The first known residents of Haiti were the Ciboney, an Indian people who originated in Central or South America and migrated to the Caribbean region about 2000 B.C.

The Ciboney settled on most of the islands of the Caribbean. Those who lived on what is now Haiti made their homes in caves and were skilled in chipping large knives and spearheads from pieces of flint. Many of these flints, as well as some ancient graves, have been discovered at the sites of former Ciboney settlements. Archaeologists (scientists who study the physical evidence of prehistoric and historic human cultures) believe that the Ciboney lived in small groups, each consisting of a few families. They hunted, fished, and gathered fruits, but they did not plant crops.

In about 300 B.C., the Ciboney way of life was disrupted by a wave of immigrants from South America. Known as the Arawak, these newcomers arrived in the Caribbean area during a great migration that lasted until about 100 A.D. Arawak culture was more elaborate than that of the Ciboney. The Arawak knew how to cultivate crops and make pottery—skills they spread everywhere they went. They also carved stone into statues, perhaps of their gods. Their settlements, much larger than the Ciboney's, were socially complex and ruled by hereditary chieftains.

The Arawak subgroup that settled in Haiti was called the Taino. Greatly outnumbering the Ciboney, the Taino people soon killed off most of the earlier residents or absorbed them through intermarriage. A small number of the Ciboney fled into remote areas in the southwest, where they kept their language and culture alive for the next several centuries. But the island remained in the hands of the Arawak until a new race of invaders—the Europeans—appeared on the scene.

The Nativity

Christopher Columbus, the Italian-born explorer, sighted the island now occupied by Haiti and the Dominican Republic on December 6, 1492. Claiming it for his sponsors, King Ferdinand and Queen Isabella of Spain, he named it La Isla Española (the Spanish Island), which was shortened to Hispaniola over the years.

The Spanish monarchs had funded Columbus's expedition after he assured them that he could find a fast new sea route to the rich eastern lands known as "the Indies." When the explorer landed in the tropical Caribbean, he believed that he was off the coast of India and that the people he encountered were, therefore, Indians. Although later explorers proved that Columbus had actually found a new—to Europe—world, his name for the area stuck. Ever since 1492, the islands of the Caribbean have been called the West Indies.

Historians estimate that between 500,000 and 1 million Taino lived on Hispaniola in 1492. Columbus, who described the Taino as "loveable, tractable, peaceable, and praiseworthy," immediately noted that many wore gold ornaments. Now he was certain that "profitable things without number" could be found in Hispaniola. He ordered his three ships, the *Niña*, the *Pinta*, and the *Santa María*, to cruise along the coast of Hispaniola for several weeks, trading with the Taino. Then disaster struck.

On Christmas Eve, 1492, Columbus's flagship, the *Santa María*, was wrecked on a reef near the present-day city of Cap-Haïtien. The

On Christmas Eve, 1492, Columbus's flagship, the Santa María, *was wrecked off Haiti's north shore. Stranded mariners formed the island's first colony.*

ship was beyond repair, and Columbus was forced to abandon it. Because the *Niña* and the *Pinta* could not accommodate the entire crew of the *Santa María*, Columbus decided to leave some of his men on Hispaniola. When the *cacique* (chief) of the nearest Taino community offered the Spanish seamen two houses in his village, Columbus accepted. He named the tiny colony La Navidad (the Spanish term for the Nativity, or birth of Christ), ordered his men to start trading with the Indians for gold, and set sail for Spain.

When he returned the following year, bringing more settlers, supplies, and ships, he found La Navidad burned to the ground. His men were dead, probably killed by Indians who had come to resent the Spaniards' lust for gold. Abandoning the ruins of La Navidad (which disappeared from view until archaeologists rediscovered it almost five centuries later) Columbus moved eastward along the coast. He founded a new settlement in what is now the Dominican Republic and in 1498 established his headquarters on the site of the present Dominican capital, Santo Domingo.

Columbus, who governed Hispaniola until 1500, faced ongoing problems with the Spanish settlers, who fought among themselves and treated the Indians brutally. When the Indians rose in revolt, Columbus sent troops to attack them, hoping to calm the angry settlers. After defeating the Indians, he established a system called *repartimiento*, which would be employed throughout Latin America for centuries. Under repartimiento, Spanish settlers were given huge tracts of land and everything on it—including Indians.

The Taino people—enslaved, treated barbarously, and exposed to deadly new diseases brought by the Europeans—were soon almost wiped out. Only half a century after Columbus landed on Hispaniola, an Indian population that had numbered between 500,000 and 1 million was reduced to 500. In the meantime, Spanish colonial administrators needed someone to do the heavy work that, as historian Samuel Eliot Morison has pointed out, "Europeans were too proud or too lazy to do." They hit on a new source of labor: black slaves from West Africa. With the arrival of slaves in Hispaniola, early in the 16th century, came the seeds of Haiti's African culture and its eventual revolt and independence.

Pirates and Plantations

Hoping to gain great wealth from Santo Domingo, Spain sent many settlers to the colony in the early 16th century. But the island was a disappointment, proving to have very little gold and no silver, gems, or spices. At the same time, however, the Spanish were acquiring fabulous riches elsewhere in the Americas: In 1521, Hernando Cortés conquered the Aztec kingdom of Mexico, and in 1536,

Francisco Pizarro completed his conquest of Peru's glittering Inca empire.

The vast deposits of gold and silver in these lands drew Spain's attention away from Santo Domingo; many Spaniards who had gone there in search of treasure moved to the mainland. By the end of the 16th century, Santo Domingo had become no more than a stopping point for ships headed for Spain with loot from the Aztecs and Incas.

Although the Spanish neglected Hispaniola, others did not. Spain's treasure fleets attracted the attention of French and English pirates, maritime bandits whose swift raiding ships trailed convoys of Spanish galleons like wolves after a herd of deer. The pirates needed safe, secret harbors where they could repair and provision their ships; the isolated islands around Hispaniola were ideal for such purposes.

In the 1620s, French pirates made a stronghold of the island of Tortuga, off Haiti's north coast. There they lay in wait for the Spanish treasure fleets sailing from Panama, and there they returned to stock their ships with fresh water and meat from the island's abundant turtles. The pirates also stole cows and pigs from settlers on other islands. They carried the animals to Tortuga, where they ran wild and bred new generations, assuring ample food supplies.

Tortuga is small and comparatively barren. Attracted to the more fertile main island, the pirates established a number of settlements in the western part of Hispaniola, an area occupied only by a handful of Spaniards and a few Arawak Indians. Between raids on the Spanish, the French hunted and even farmed. The Arawak taught them how to cure meat by smoking it on frameworks of green wood called *boucans*. From this word came *buccaneers*, the term used for the Caribbean pirates of the 17th century.

Despite Spanish opposition, increasing numbers of French pirate-farmers settled in the western part of Hispaniola, which they

King Louis XIV brought part of the colony under French control in 1664.

called Saint-Domingue. When Spain, enmeshed both in European wars and in conflicts in the New World, proved unable to drive the French out, King Louis XIV of France decided to make the most of the situation. In 1664, he authorized the French West India Company to take control of Saint-Domingue.

The French company established its headquarters on the northwest coast, naming the settlement Port-de-Paix. Appointed governor of the new colony was a former pirate named Bertrand d'Ogeron, who sent to France for young peasant women to marry the pirates-turned-colonists and to Africa for more black slaves to work the land. Cap-Français, which would become the French colony's capital, was founded in 1670 on the site of present-day Cap-Haïtien. By the end of the 17th century, France was the dominant power in northwestern Hispaniola.

In 1697, decades of European warfare were concluded with the Treaty of Ryswick. Under the terms of the treaty, Spain formally gave France the territory—then officially called Saint-Domingue—that would become the nation of Haiti. The century of the great plantations had begun.

Eager to make their fortunes in the New World, French colonists flocked to Saint-Domingue. There, they carved out huge estates in the Northern Plain and the Artibonite Plain, raising coffee, cacao (the beans used to make chocolate), cotton, indigo (a plant that yields a blue dye greatly prized in the 18th century), and—most important—sugarcane. Sugar would make Saint-Domingue the richest colony in the Americas and the richest French colony in the world. In 1789, two-thirds of all France's overseas investments were in Saint-Domingue, which shipped more than 120 million pounds of sugar to France in a good year. More than 700 ships and 80,000 seamen were needed to handle the colony's sugar trade.

All this wealth was paid for by human suffering. Several million black slaves worked on the plantations of Saint-Domingue over the

A French soldier trains caged bloodhounds to track the scent of runaway slaves.

course of the 18th century. The death toll—from disease, overwork, and brutal treatment—was staggering. Historians believe, in fact, that so many slaves died that planters replaced the entire slave population every 20 years. Most of the slaves, purchased at the port of Ouidah, the capital of Dahomey in West Africa, were related to the ancestors of people now living in Nigeria, Ghana, and other West African nations. Later in the century, some slaves were brought to Saint-Domingue from the Congo region of Central Africa.

The intermingling of white French landowners and black slaves soon gave rise to a third population group: mulattoes, or people of mixed (black and white) parentage. The first mulattoes were the children of white planter fathers and black slave mothers. Laws passed in 1685 granted freedom to some of these people, who were known as *gens de couleur* (people of color) or *affranchis* (freemen).

The free mulattoes established themselves as a separate social class, living among and marrying only members of their own group. Many entered business or agriculture, and some became extremely wealthy, able to buy both plantations and slaves. Adopting the values of the French landowners, mulattoes generally prized French language and culture and often became Roman Catholics.

Early in the 18th century, Saint-Domingue's white population treated the free mulattoes as equals. Mulattoes sent their children to school in France as the whites did, and the two racial groups mingled in church and social affairs. But many whites became uneasy about the increasing wealth and prestige of the mulattoes; some feared they might try to take over the colony. Aiming to keep the mulattoes under control, the white-run colonial government passed new, restrictive laws. Starting about 1760, free mulattoes were forbidden to carry weapons, enter certain professions, or marry whites. They were also required to wear special identifying clothing and sit in segregated parts of churches and theaters. Predictably, these laws created deep resentment among the mulattoes.

In 1789, on the eve of the French Revolution, Saint-Domingue's population consisted of some 500,000 black slaves, 32,000 whites, and 24,000 mulattoes. The three groups shared little but mutual hostility: Blacks hated their white masters; whites feared and exploited their black slaves; mulattoes detested and were detested by both blacks and whites. The stage was set for violent confrontation.

Born a slave, Toussaint L'Ouverture was one of the leaders of the slave revolt of 1791. He later became an officer in the Spanish army and governor-general of Haiti.

Revolt and Independence

The outbreak of the French Revolution in 1789 brought unrest to Saint-Domingue. The colony's white aristocrats, alarmed by the new-found power of France's lower classes, wanted to declare the colony independent of France. The free mulattoes hoped the revolution would bring them a fair share of rights and privileges. And the slaves, brutally mistreated for so many years, were ready to unleash their rage against their masters.

The violence began in 1790, when the French revolutionary government decreed that any colonial property owner over the age of 25 could vote. The Saint-Domingue administration, however, announced that the law did not apply to mulattoes, whom it termed a "bastard and degenerate race." Reacting in fury, the mulattoes, led by 40-year-old Jacques Vincent Ogé, staged a revolt against the government. Ogé was captured, tortured, and executed, but the fire he had ignited continued to burn. In the north, slaves began the revolution that the rulers of Saint-Domingue had dreaded for centuries.

The rebellion was set in motion by a slave named Boukman, who served as overseer on a huge plantation near Cap-Haïtien. For months, he had been secretly communicating with the 12,000 slaves in the Cap-Haïtien area, preparing for the day when they would

France lost its grip on the island forever when the French army was defeated in 1803.

smash the system that kept them in bondage. On the stormy night of August 22, 1791, that day arrived. Shouting "Vengeance!" slaves from all over the north surged forth to burn plantations to the ground and slaughter their inhabitants. As historian C. L. R. James has observed of the slaves, "From their masters they had known rape, torture, degradation, and, at the slightest provocation, death. They returned in kind."

Soon after the revolt began, Boukman was captured and beheaded by government forces. His place as rebel leader was taken by a freed slave named François-Dominique Toussaint L'Ouverture, one of three great black leaders (along with Jean-Jacques Dessalines and Henri Christophe) who rose to prominence during the slave rebellion. A skilled military strategist, Toussaint taught his forces guerrilla warfare, a fighting style that proved highly effective against the regimented French army. Under Toussaint, the flames of revolution continued to race through the nation.

Joining the battle were many mulattoes, who put aside their traditional hatred for the blacks to help defeat the common enemy. Help also came from hidden communities of *maroons*, escaped slaves living in remote mountainous areas, who hunted by day and raided plantations by night. The combined forces were irresistible. A few

But Christophe's most stunning monument—still standing on a mountaintop just south of Sans Souci—is the Citadelle La Ferrière, a massive stone fortress built as a defense against Napoléon. Its construction, which took 13 years, required the forced labor of 200,000 workers. Some 20,000 men lost their life in the process, which involved hauling huge blocks of stone and 600 weighty brass cannons up the steep mountain slopes, accessible even today only on foot or horseback. Some Haitians say the fortress remains standing because the blood of those workers was mixed into the mortar between the building blocks. Fearful that enemies would learn secret details of the citadel's design, Christophe reportedly imprisoned the architects in deep dungeons beneath it.

Despite Christophe's fears, none of the citadel's cannons ever fired a shot. The French never came back to Haiti. Instead, Christophe's own subjects rose in rebellion against him and his iron-handed rule. In 1820, as a peasant army marched to capture him, Christophe shot himself in the throne room of Sans Souci. According to legend, he used a silver bullet—the only missile that could kill him. His remains still lie in the fort's courtyard, buried under a bronze tablet that reads, "I will be reborn from my ashes." Christophe has not kept that promise, but his mighty citadel is now being restored by the United Nations as a World Heritage Site, one of many natural or historic sites around the world maintained by

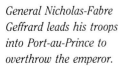

General Nicholas-Fabre Geffrard leads his troops into Port-au-Prince to overthrow the emperor.

funds from the United Nations Educational, Scientific, and Cultural Organization.

Years of Turmoil

Meanwhile, Pétion had set up a republic in the south. Well-educated and politically moderate, he allowed his people greater freedom than those who lived under Christophe's rule. Like their northern neighbors, however, the residents of the south were forced to work long, hard hours in the field in order to survive.

Pétion died in 1818. Succeeding him as president in the southern part of Haiti was Jean-Pierre Boyer, a mulatto who had been educated in France. Boyer became president of the whole country after Christophe's death in 1820, and in 1822 he brought the entire island under his control by invading and conquering Santo Domingo, in Hispaniola's eastern sector. When the country's economy continued to deteriorate, Boyer adopted the harsh tactics of Dessalines and Christophe, driving his countrymen to work under armed guard. Boyer was overthrown in 1843; a year later, the Santo Domingans drove the Haitians from their territory and renamed the eastern part of the island the Dominican Republic.

Between 1843 and 1915, Haiti occasionally experienced periods of peace and progress, but these years were more often marked by turmoil. Conflicts continued between impoverished blacks and mulattoes, who remained the nation's wealthiest citizens, and leaders regularly rose and fell. Of the era's 22 rulers, most of them black army officers, 14 were overthrown by revolution, 2 were assassinated, and 1 was killed by an explosion in his palace (which also served as the nation's chief ammunition depot).

The army placed four blacks in the presidency between 1844 and 1859. One was Faustin-Élie Soulouque, who declared himself emperor, killed many mulattoes, and launched two unsuccessful invasions of the Dominican Republic. Soulouque was driven out of the

(continued on p. 65)

Scenes of
HAITI

◄ Small tin-roofed houses like this one usually belong to the more prosperous members of a rural community; other rural Haitians live in huts of woven sticks, scrap boards, and thatched palm leaves.

∀ Port-au-Prince's two-block-long Iron Market is named for its buildings of painted wrought iron.

nd ∧ *Many blacks are drawn to the cities in search of jobs, but most find only poverty and unemployment. Thousands of them live in slums and shantytowns with skyrocketing rates of disease, malnutrition, and crime.*

⋀ and ⋁ A stream serves as a communal laundry and bathing center. Many Haitians also
depend upon such streams for drinking water. Sewers often flow into the
streams, however, and most communities do not have sewage treatment or water
purification plants. Unsafe drinking water is a leading cause of disease.

⋏ *These fishermen using a hand-held net will probably bring home a few fish to feed their families or to sell in a local market. With proper equipment and training, experts believe, Haiti's fishermen could reap a large commercial harvest from the sea.*

∧ *Cacti and weeds thrive in stony, dry regions beyond the grasslands.*

◄ *Erosion has carved gullies down thousands of bare, scorched hillsides.*

⋏ *Patches of Haiti's original rain forest survive in the south.*

ʌ *The view from this lonely highland homestead could have inspired the Haitian saying, "Beyond the mountains, more mountains."*

country by Nicholas-Fabre Geffrard, who served as president from 1859 to 1867. Geffrard is remembered for his public works: He built water reservoirs, founded gaslight companies, opened libraries and schools, and made peace with the Roman Catholic church, which then sent teachers and missionaries to Haiti. Florvil Hyppolite, president from 1889 to 1896, was another reformer. A builder of bridges and markets, he was also responsible for bringing telegraph and telephone service to Haiti.

During these years, revolution became big business in Haiti. Most of the nation's presidents were installed by armies of mercenaries (soldiers who fight strictly for money, rather than for patriotic or nationalistic reasons). These free-lance "kingmakers" were known as *cacos*. A would-be president could borrow money from a merchant (usually at 100 percent interest, to be paid after a successful revolution) and hire an army of cacos. In return for a cash payment and permission to loot towns on their march to the capital, the cacos would overthrow the current head of state and install their employer in his place.

For the first few years after it became independent in 1804, small, strife-torn Haiti received little attention from the outside world. But over the years, a few countries finally extended diplomatic recognition to the Caribbean republic: France in 1825, Great Britain in 1833, and the United States in 1862. In order to build a fueling station for American naval vessels, the United States rented land near Cap-Haïtien from the Haitian government in the late 1860s.

Haiti's civil unrest and political instability reached a peak between 1908 and 1915: The country had seven presidents in seven years. This tumultuous era ended in July 1915, soon after the seventh president, Vilbrun Guillaume Sam, had marched into Port-au-Prince at the head of a caco army. Learning that a political rival was headed for the capital with another caco army, Sam imprisoned 167 supporters of his opponent and fled into the French embassy. When the

United States Marines prepare an artillery position outside Port-au-Prince in 1915.

prisoners were murdered, probably on Sam's orders, an infuriated mob broke into the embassy, hacked the short-term president to pieces, and paraded through the streets with his remains.

At this point, the United States intervened in Haiti's domestic affairs. World War I was under way in Europe, and Haiti's position on the Windward Passage had become important. America feared that Germany, which had many warships in the Caribbean, would seize control of strategically situated Haiti, from which it could harass ships passing through the Panama Canal. Using the murder of President Sam as its official motive, the United States sent the marines to invade and occupy Haiti.

After the invasion, Haitians were forced to accept a treaty that gave the United States full power over their financial and military affairs. The American administration of Haiti was often high-handed, going so far as to create a new Haitian constitution without consulting the Haitians. But the Americans were also responsible for substantial reforms in the battered island nation. U.S. officials helped to balance Haiti's budget and reduce corruption, and U.S. engineers built schools, roads, hospitals, sewage plants, and reservoirs.

No amount of good works, however, could keep the Haitians from resenting the Americans' uninvited presence. Particularly bitter toward the United States were the cacos, who were suddenly out of work. When the marines began drafting farmers for road-building labor, a large force of these free-lance soldiers tried to stage a nationwide revolt against the U.S. occupation. The U.S. Marines quickly stamped out the rebellion, effectively eliminating the cacos as a source of disorder. General opposition to the Americans, however, continued.

In 1930, U.S. president Herbert Hoover decided that it was time to reduce American forces in Haiti. In an election supervised by the marines, Sténio Vincent, a mulatto, was chosen as the nation's president. Although President Franklin D. Roosevelt withdrew the last marines from Haiti in 1934, the United States retained control of Haiti's finances until 1947.

Vincent remained in office until 1941. The major event of his presidency was a bloody conflict with the neighboring Dominican Republic. Although many Dominicans, proud of their Spanish heritage, looked down on the African-descended Haitians, the Dominican economy depended on low-paid migrant workers from Haiti. But in 1937, claiming that large numbers of Haitians were illegally entering and settling in the Republic, the Dominicans massacred thou-

Sténio Vincent, a mulatto, was president from 1930 until 1941.

Dumarsais Estimé, a black, was made president by the army, which overthrew him four years later.

sands of them along the border. After appealing to an inter-American commission, Vincent forced the Dominican Republic to pay a large sum in compensation for the murdered Haitians.

Vincent's successor, Élie Lescot, was also a mulatto. But by now, the nation's black majority had come to resent mulatto rule, and in 1946, the army forced Lescot out of office and installed a black, Dumarsais Estimé, as president. Four years later, when Estimé tried to change the constitution so he could remain in power, he, too, was overthrown by the army.

The next president, General Paul Magloire, was another army choice. He was said to be highly corrupt, but he improved the country's economy by promoting foreign trade and investment. In the end, Magloire made the same mistake as his predecessor: He attempted to extend his term of office illegally. He was ousted by the military in December 1956. During the following nine months, seven governments were formed, but each fell apart almost immediately. The time was ripe for a strong leader who could win the support of the people and the army. Such a man appeared in September 1957.

President Paul Magloire delivers an inaugural speech after the army made him president in 1950.

The Duvaliers

François Duvalier was born in 1907 and received a medical degree from the Haiti School of Medicine. Nicknamed "Papa Doc," he served as minister of public health and labor under President Estimé. Stepping up his political activity, he helped drive Magloire from office in 1956. When he was elected president in September 1957, Duvalier proceeded to establish a firm grip on the reins of government.

First, he created the Tontons Macoutes, a private force of secret police and terrorists assigned to carry out his orders. Tonton Macoutes, which means "Uncle Knapsack," comes from a sinister figure of Haitian folklore who seizes naughty children and carries them away in his bag. All Duvalier's Tontons Macoutes wore identical clothing: blue suits, open-necked white shirts, and dark glasses. Before long, this "uniform" was respected—and feared—throughout the land.

Well aware that most of his predecessors had been overthrown by the army, Duvalier next reduced the military's size and power.

The Tontons Macoutes, Duvalier's private police force, wielded enormous power.

Then he ordered all his opponents imprisoned or killed by the Tontons Macoutes. Although he had been raised a Catholic, he strengthened his hold on the Haitian people by publicizing his belief in Voodoo, the African-based religion practiced by most of the nation's black population. Duvalier always dressed in a black suit, wore sunglasses, and spoke in a quiet voice—habits that made him resemble the Voodoo lord of the graveyard, Baron Samedi, who is always depicted as a somberly clothed undertaker. In time, many Haitians believed that Papa Doc *was* Baron Samedi, a supernatural being with powers of life and death over everyone.

In 1964, Duvalier abolished Haiti's constitution and declared himself president for life. By this time Haiti was a police state, with Papa Doc its sole source of power. Many countries, including the United States, suspended aid to Haiti because of its president's corruption and tyranny. Citing Duvalier's mistreatment of clergymen, Pope Paul VI excommunicated him from the Roman Catholic church in 1966. The dictator's brutal rule inspired numerous attempts to overthrow or assassinate him, but none succeeded: Papa Doc remained in power until his death in 1971. He had named his son, Jean-Claude Duvalier, as his successor.

The younger Duvalier, who was known as "Baby Doc," took over as president for life in 1971. Only 19 years old at the time, he was the youngest president in the world. The United States and other countries urged him to soften some of his father's harsh policies, and at first he appeared to comply, releasing some political prisoners and relaxing government censorship of the press. But although young Duvalier seemed more liberal than his father had been, he was just as determined to retain complete control of the country. When political opposition arose, the Tontons Macoutes appeared in the streets.

In 1980, Duvalier married Michèle Bennett, a beautiful young Haitian woman who had been educated in the United States. Newspapers around the world printed photographs of the couple's wedding—which, at a cost of $3 million, was one of the most expensive ever held anywhere—next to pictures of starving Haitian children. After their marriage, the Duvaliers combined a wildly extravagant personal life with repressive, corrupt rule. Observed by a people in

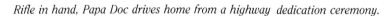

Rifle in hand, Papa Doc drives home from a highway dedication ceremony.

The lavish wedding of Baby Doc Duvalier and Michèle Bennett stirred anger among Haiti's poor.

the grip of steadily increasing poverty, the couple's undisguised greed soon created a nationwide wave of anger.

As Haiti's economic downslide accelerated, rumors began to circulate: The Voodoo spirits, it was said, were angry with the president and his wife. Protests against the couple were answered by police crackdowns and beatings, but popular anger continued to smolder, and Haitians from many levels of society—students, workers, and army officers—joined the anti-Duvalier movement.

In February 1986, that movement erupted. Clubs and bullets flew as rioters battled police officers and Tontons Macoutes across the nation. When the Duvaliers realized they could count on little support from the army and none from the common people, they fled to France, taking with them millions of dollars in plundered government funds. The couple's departure, said the Roman Catholic bishop of Cap-Haïtien, was Haiti's "second independence."

Chaos and Hope

A military council, under General Henri Namphy, took immediate charge of the country. Namphy dissolved the National Assembly but also said that the military would disband the Tontons Macoutes, create a new constitution, institute reforms, and then turn the country over to the people. The nation's citizens rejoiced, but conditions did not improve, and it soon became clear that many of those now in power were Duvalier sympathizers.

Amid a flurry of demonstrations, Namphy announced that elections would be held and a new constitution—the nation's 23rd since independence in 1804—would be drawn up. In 1987, voters approved the constitution, which introduced a democratic governmental structure and contained provisions aimed at preventing the return of dictatorship. The promised election, however, proved a disaster, as gunmen—possibly directed by Namphy—burned election headquarters and killed 34 voters. Namphy rescheduled elections for 1988. Fear kept most voters home, but university professor and anti-Duvalierist Leslie Manigat was elected president.

When Manigat attempted to have Namphy arrested for refusing to cooperate in reorganizing the army, troops loyal to Namphy staged yet another coup, returning him to power for several months of murder and arson under the Tontons Macoutes. After another general, Prosper Avril, a Duvalierist, ousted Namphy, rioting mobs killed sus-

Jean-Bertrand Aristide, left, embraces his successor, René Préval, at the new president's inauguration in February 1996. Préval wears the presidential sash.

pected Tontons Macoutes in the streets. Avril promised to uphold the constitution and to hold elections within three years. In a rare gesture for Haitian politics, he kept these promises. In 1990, a charismatic Jesuit priest with enormous popular following, Jean-Bertrand Aristide, was easily elected president in what foreign observers called a fair and free election.

Once it became clear, however, that Aristide intended fundamental reforms which would transfer power to the impoverished majority, he too was overthrown in a military coup, followed by an extended bloodbath. Over the next three years, tens of thousands of Haitians attempted to escape to the United States in small boats, leading to a disaster of another kind as many drowned at sea or were picked up by the U.S. Coast Guard and placed under quarantine in Florida. Haiti, it seemed, had sunk to a new low in its disastrous history of maltreatment of the population.

Aristide, exiled by the military, took refuge in the United States and kept his case before the public. When international diplomacy failed to secure his return, the United Nations, under prodding by the United States, imposed increasingly harsh embargoes and economic sanctions on Haiti to force the hand of the military. Finally, in late 1994, after a series of broken agreements by a succession of sham Haitian governments, Aristide was returned to power with slightly over a year left in his presidency. This took place, however, only after a multinational force of U.N. troops,

When democracy returned to Haiti, U.N. troops remained in Port-au-Prince to preserve stability.

led by the United States, had already massed to invade Haiti. Instead, the U.N. troops entered the island as a peacekeeping force to prevent further violence and bloodshed.

Elections held in 1995 produced a countrywide landslide for Aristide's Lavalas party, with René Préval, Aristide's first prime minister, chosen as president. The U.N. troops, gradually reduced in number from a high of about 20,000, took on the difficult task of retraining the military and the national police as nonpolitical professional forces, rather than instruments of terror. In addition, large amounts of money, in the form of direct grants and loans, poured into the country, and volunteers staffed numerous agencies set up by both the United Nations and individual national governments to improve the economic, legal, and health systems of the devastated country.

Though most Haitians pray to Christ and the saints, they merge their version of Christianity with the African traditions of Voodoo.

Government and Economy

The 1987 Haitian constitution formed the basis for the first fully democratic government Haiti had ever known. Although the interference of the military, through a succession of coups and counter-coups, delayed its implementation, it took hold in the late 1990s—but only after the threat of intervention from the United States and other members of the United Nations. Predicting the future of Haiti is a risky business at any time, but at last it seems that the will of the people has been heard and acted upon.

Under the constitution, all men and women over age 18 have voting rights. Because so many Haitians are illiterate, however, many elections in the past have been fraudulent. In the 1964 election, when François Duvalier "ran" for the post of president for life, he was the only candidate. The ballots were already printed with the word Yes. A voter who wrote No could be arrested for defacing a ballot. In 1971, the ailing Duvalier called for a national referendum, asking the people to approve his choice of Baby Doc as his successor. The official results of the referendum released by the presidential palace were 2.5 million yes votes, one no vote. Such an electoral history has made Haitians understandably suspicious of the voting process.

An armed soldier patrols a Port-au-Prince voting place in January 1988.

Haiti is divided into nine provinces, or *départements*. The departement capitals are: Hinche, Jérémie, Gonaïves, Cap-Haïtien, Fort-Liberté, Port-de-Paix, Port-au-Prince, Les Cayes, and Jacmel. Each province is divided into *communes*, or counties, and further subdivided into *bourgs*, or townships. There are also several rural districts that are not divided into communes and bourgs because they contain only scattered settlements.

Haiti's judicial system follows the traditional French model, and many of its laws are based on the Napoleonic Code. The nation's highest court is the Court of Cassation, which sits in Port-au-Prince and functions much like the U.S. Supreme Court. Each département has its own civil and criminal courts, and each of the bourgs has a justice of the peace. Special courts deal with cases involving juveniles, property rights, military matters, and labor disputes.

About 4,000 people serve in Haiti's armed forces. The army is by far the largest military branch; Haiti has a small navy and a still smaller air force. The armed forces are responsible for security and order throughout the country; local detachments serve as police. Although Port-au-Prince has its own police department, it is under

The people who danced in the streets after the Duvaliers fled soon encountered new problems under a succession of military governments.

the central government and in the past has been used by dictatorial regimes to control the population. The dreaded Tontons Macoutes, the secret police, were officially disbanded after the fall of the Duvaliers, but remained an oppressive behind-the-scenes force until suppressed by the United Nations troops, who also forced the removal of many military and police personnel.

Resources and Economy

Haiti's natural resources are limited. Gold was discovered along the Haitian-Dominican frontier in the 16th century, but very little remains today. Bauxite, a mineral used in the manufacture of aluminum, has been profitably mined in the southern peninsula since the 1950s, but in recent years, the world demand for bauxite has declined. Deposits of silver, manganese, copper, and coal have been discovered, but few are extensive enough for commercial exploitation. Limestone, sand, and gravel are mined throughout the island for construction purposes. No reserves of oil or natural gas have yet been found in Haiti or its offshore waters.

Just as it was in colonial times, agriculture is Haiti's economic mainstay. Together, farming and livestock raising occupy 50 percent of the land, accounting for 35 percent of the country's economic

Plantation workers dry sisal fibers in the sun. The plant fibers are used to make ropes.

production. A few large plantations, owned by corporations or by the state, use hired laborers to cultivate sugarcane and rice. Most of the sugar is exported; most of the rice is consumed at home. Other export crops include coffee, sisal (a fiber used in making rope), bananas, and cacao. These crops are raised on small plots by independent farmers, who carry them to market and sell them to dealers or brokers. Although the brokers often make a good deal of money selling to foreign markets, the farmers usually make very little. Farmers in the south grow aromatic plants that are prized by perfume makers; these include lime, vetiver, neroli, and amyris.

Nearly everyone who lives outside the cities—about 70 percent of the population—works on the land, if only to grow fruits and vegetables for family use. The most common of these subsistence crops are sweet potatoes, rice, peas, beans, cassava (a starchy plant whose root is used for making flour), mangoes, corn, okra (a vegetable of African origin), plantains (starchy cooking bananas), and peanuts. Most families grow some sugarcane for their own use. Haitian farmers also raise cattle, pigs, goats, and chickens, but the quality of the livestock is generally poor because the animals feed on scrub vegetation. Cattle and pigs are kept mainly on large commercial farms; typical farmers are more likely to have a few goats or chickens.

Although the people of Haiti's many small coastal villages support themselves by fishing, the country has no organized fishing industry. Most boats and equipment are primitive and inefficient, and fishermen usually catch only enough to feed their families or sell in a local market. Still, experts believe that Haiti's waters could support a profitable fishing industry once money becomes available for equipment and training.

Haiti's small local factories produce items such as cement, baseballs, toys, beverages, shoes, and electronic components. Some, baseballs and electronic equipment in particular, are exported, and the rest retained for domestic sales. Haiti's principal trading partners are the United States, France, Taiwan, Germany, Italy, Japan, and Belgium. The country buys petroleum from the Netherlands Antilles, a group of Caribbean islands.

Before the United Nations imposed economic sanctions, "assembly" plants—factories that assemble parts, often foreign-made, into finished products—had been a growing industry. The sanctions virtually destroyed production, however, which is slowly returning under the democratic administration. The Préval government has sought to improve and stabilize the economy by controlling the budget, easing regulations, and selling many inefficient government-owned industries to private corporations.

The national currency is the *gourde*, divided into 100 *centimes*. Recently, 15–20 gourdes have been equal to 1 U.S. dollar. The average annual income in Haiti is $340, the lowest in the Western Hemisphere. The figure is misleading, however, because a few wealthy Haitians make a great deal more than the average, and the poorest farmers live almost entirely outside the cash economy. These farmers use the barter system, trading vegetables or chickens for such items as water, clothing, medical supplies, and tools.

Some rural Haitians practice such crafts as boat building, basket weaving, or sewing (by hand or with old-fashioned, foot-operated machines). Almost everyone tries to raise a few extra vegetables or chickens to sell for a gourde or two at the nearest marketplace. Nevertheless, few country people earn enough money for such "luxuries" as medical treatment or books.

In the country, most people work at something, even if it is only tilling a tiny plot of land. In the towns and cities, however, unemployment is high. Factory jobs are scarce in Haiti, and tourism, once the economy's fastest-growing sector, has virtually disappeared, taking many jobs with it. Fortunate city dwellers sometimes find work as street vendors; others work as scavengers, gathering old tin cans to sell to scrap-metal dealers, or collecting cardboard and discarded plastic wrapping to peddle in the markets.

Transportation

Until the U.S. Marines began building roads in 1915, all travel in Haiti was on foot or horseback. Today, Haiti's impoverished majority still travels on foot. *Tap-taps*, pickup trucks that have been converted into informal buses, are found in many rural areas. Although brightly painted and adorned with names such as "Mother of God" and "Jesus Before All," the tap-taps are rickety and dangerous. No organized public-transportation service is available. People who want to travel

Country people hope to sell their goods for cash at rural markets, but often they simply trade them for items they need.

Brightly painted buses called tap-taps *offer informal public transportation in rural areas.*

between towns arrange for rides in tap-taps or other trucks; those who can afford it take taxis in Port-au-Prince and Cap-Haïtien.

Haiti now has 2,500 miles (4,000 kilometers) of roads, about one-quarter of which are paved. The unpaved roads tend to dissolve into muddy swamps in the rainy season and turn into dusty, bone-jarring trails when the weather is dry. Many country roads are bisected by streams, but bridges are rare; travelers must risk crossing at treacherous fords. Small communities in the interior are often linked only by footpaths.

A single short stretch of railway connected several of the large sugarcane plantations to the harbor at Port-au-Prince, but was closed in 1990. There is no passenger-train service. Port-au-Prince is the main seaport, with Cap-Haïtien, Gonaïves, and Jacmel also serving as ports for trading vessels. Local traders use sailboats and motorboats to serve the needs of many coastal villages that cannot be reached overland.

If he cannot scratch a living from the land, this young man may join the flight to the cities.

People and Ways of Life

The pattern of today's Haitian society was set during the French colonial era, when the nation's population consisted primarily of French whites and African blacks. At the end of the colonial period, a third group, the light-skinned mulattoes, chose to adopt French customs and values. From that time on, Haitian society has been divided between the mulattoes and the blacks.

The mulattoes, most of whom lived in Port-au-Prince, were characterized by wealth, education, the Roman Catholic religion, and the use of French language. Even after they lost political power, they retained most of the country's wealth. Through a complex network of family relationships and private clubs, they also controlled the nation's elite social and cultural life.

Most of the blacks, on the other hand, were poor rural farmers with little or no education. Their ways of life were close to those in West African cultures, and they practiced the Voodoo religion. Their language was Creole, which combines French, Spanish, and African words, and uses African-style pronunciation and sentence structure. Although French is a component of Creole, few blacks could understand French. Most French-speaking mulattoes, however, could speak Creole. As a result, communication between a black and a mulatto was controlled by the mulatto.

The Port-au-Prince Cathedral is a symbol of Haiti's official religion, Roman Catholicism.

In recent years, the dividing line between Haiti's blacks and mulattoes has begun to blur. Many blacks have arrived at positions of political power, earning them a place in the nation's elite society. At the same time, some blacks have become quite wealthy, and some mulatto families have become less so. A well-known Haitian proverb expresses the relationship between money and social status: "A rich black is a mulatto; a poor mulatto is a black." Black Haitian culture has found new expression in literature and art, and some mulattoes have begun to take pride in their African heritage. French remains the official language, but Creole, the language of the peasant masses, is now accepted for use in the courts and in some schools.

Today, Haiti's population is about 95 percent black and 5 percent mulatto; a few whites of foreign descent also live in Haiti, most of them in Port-au-Prince. Urban mulattoes have their own distinct way of life; urban blacks have another, and the rural blacks—70 percent of the population—have yet another.

Haiti's mulattoes are city dwellers. Some are wealthy by inheritance; others work in business or the legal or medical professions. Few women of the elite mulatto class hold jobs, although a handful work as secretaries. Mulattoes own most of Haiti's 34,000 private cars, many of which are such expensive makes as Mercedes-Benz and BMW. Most mulatto children are educated in Paris, where they receive frequent visits from their well-traveled parents. People in this group often enjoy tennis and golf at private clubs. Their homes are usually large villas dating from colonial times or modern houses similar to those in wealthy sections of U.S. and European cities. These residences are situated in the suburb of Pétionville or in the hills to the east of Port-au-Prince, from which point their occupants have a splendid view of the harbor.

Members of Port-au-Prince's mulatto elite dress well, as a rule favoring fashionable European designers. They also eat well: A typical Pétionville meal might include a classic French dish or a French-influenced Haitian specialty such as spiced shrimp, green turtle steak, or pheasant with orange sauce. Heart-of-palm salad, which requires the cutting down of a tree, is a popular side dish.

Some well-to-do urban blacks enjoy similarly luxurious lives, but most belong to the middle or lower classes. Although Creole is the universal language of this group, many of its members also speak

This street vendor in Port-au-Prince manufactures ice-cream by hand.

(or at least understand) French, and an increasing number of them speak English. Urban blacks usually dress in European styles, but their garments are often homemade or purchased from used-clothing vendors. Educated middle-class blacks, most of whom live in rented apartments or small houses, work as shopkeepers, teachers, businessmen, or lawyers.

Poorer blacks are factory workers, street vendors, domestic servants, or carpenters. Many unemployed urban blacks live in slums that have grown up around the cities. The poorest of these slums, on the fringes of Port-au-Prince, goes by the ironic name of Cité Soleil (Sun City). Its inhabitants, who live in cardboard huts on a sewage-soaked landfill, have no electricity, water, or even primitive sanitary facilities.

Urban blacks now compose about 25 percent of Haiti's population. As more and more people leave the countryside for the city, this group is expected to grow faster than any other. It depends heavily on public-welfare programs for food, medicine, and other needs supplied by a broad array of international volunteers, a temporary solution at best.

By far the largest number of Haitians falls into the third population category: rural peasants. The few members of this group who have managed to accumulate a little money or local power are called

Stick-and-thatch huts called cailles *are similar to those found in West Africa.*

Hard-working donkeys carry loads of produce as well as passengers.

gros negs (big noses) or *gros habitants* (big shots). The remaining country people are extremely poor, although they may be better off than the poorest urban blacks; at least they have plots of land and can try to support themselves.

Land is the most prized commodity in the Haitian countryside, where social life is governed by a complicated system of traditions and rituals concerned with land use and ownership. Individual family plots, which the Haitians call "gardens" rather than "farms," are usually quite small. And they keep getting smaller, because Haitian tradition calls for a father to divide his land among his sons. Over the years, these holdings have been divided again and again until many are not large enough to support a family. Only a few gros habitants have farms of more than an acre. In the most crowded regions, some families struggle to survive on plots of one-fortieth of an acre, a patch measuring 33 feet by 33 feet (one-hundredth of a hectare).

Because of this crowding, the traditions that have governed country life for generations are beginning to break down. For example, an oldest son may refuse to share his father's land with his brothers, forcing them to dispute possession with him or move to a town in search of work. Land ownership in Haiti is a matter of tradition rather than of law. The country has never been completely measured by surveying instruments, and few rural Haitians hold legal titles to their property. They maintain their claim to it by occupying and using it and by the agreement of their communities. For this reason, Haitians who can make a living on their land seldom leave it for any length of time: If they are gone too long, someone else might try to take it.

Life on a Haitian farm consists of much labor and little reward, a fact that inspired an old country saying: "If work were a good thing, the rich would have taken to it long ago." The typical Haitian farmer toils from sunup to sundown, laboring on one, two, or even three small plots that may be some distance from one another. Because every scrap of fertile soil is tilled, even on steep mountainsides, country folklore is full of tragic tales about farmers falling from their fields to their death.

Tractors and other modern agricultural equipment are found only on the large commercial farms; in the countryside, even ox-drawn plows are rare. The commonest tools are machetes, digging sticks, hoes, and axes. Farmers usually plant as many different crops as they can, sometimes alternating rows of coffee bushes and fruit trees, or beans and sweet potatoes in the same garden.

Each member of a Haitian farm family has certain tasks: The man does the field work, the woman prepares the food and carries extra produce to market, and the children herd the family livestock and chase crows and rats away from the crops. For bigger jobs, such as clearing a field or building a house, a farmer may call on his *combite*, an informal work organization found throughout the rural districts. Combite members help one another in exchange for parties after the work is done; the host provides food, drink, and music for the festivities, which may last through the night.

In many ways, life among the blacks of rural Haiti resembles life in West Africa. The first slaves who came to Haiti built shelters for themselves in the style they had used at home: walls made of sticks plastered together with mud and roofs of thatched straw or palm leaves. These simple dwellings, called *cailles*, are still the most common type of housing in the countryside, although small homes built of white-painted cement blocks are also found in every community.

In the Haitian countryside, as in many parts of West Africa, men and women live together in an arrangement called *plaçage*. A form of common-law marriage, plaçage allows a man to have more than one mate and family if he can support them. The system also makes it socially acceptable for either a man or a woman to have more than one sexual partner.

Food and dress in the country are simple. Eaten in the evening, the main meal of the day usually consists of stew or rice and beans, vegetables, and fruit. Wheat flour is unheard of in the country; instead, farm women make their bread from corn, cassava, or peanuts. Country dwellers consume sugar raw from the cane, in the form of a thick syrup called *rapadou*, and in *clairin*, a homemade rum. Men and women alike wear broad-brimmed straw hats. Men wear shorts and shirts, and women wear dresses, usually sewn at home from purchased fabric. Material for clothing is a major expense for most rural families.

Health and Education

The Haitian health system is extremely inadequate for the country's population. Only about 1,100 doctors practice in Haiti, most in Port-au-Prince, and there is only one hospital bed for every 1,200 citizens. Most hospitals and clinics are located in the larger cities, though increased international concern has led to foreign sponsorship of rural clinics. The question remains whether the Haitian government can keep these institutions running once outside funding is reduced.

Haitian schools train doctors, dentists, and nurses, but their graduates often leave the country to practice in Canada, the United

States, or Europe because of higher salaries and greater prestige. In recent years, however, there has been a movement among young doctors to practice medicine where they are most needed: in their own country's rural districts and city slums.

Malnutrition remains Haiti's most serious health problem. Many babies and children die from lack of nourishing food, and those who survive are weakened and likely to fall victim to other illnesses. The infant mortality rate in Haiti is high: more than 100 of every 1,000 children die during their first year, and life expectancy is more than 20 years below that in the United States.

The most common fatal illnesses among adults are malaria, tuberculosis, and dysentery, a contagious disease that causes severe diarrhea. Dysentery, like many other ailments prevalent in Haiti, is largely the result of the nation's poor sanitation and impure drinking water. Many districts have no sewage systems, and less than a quarter of the population has access to filtered water. The country has some leprosy cases but no organized program to treat them.

Since 1981, AIDS has also been a serious health problem in Haiti, though it has not proved to be the irresistible plague that was first feared. Throughout the world, AIDS has spread most readily among intravenous drug users and people with multiple sexual partners. Despite intensive worldwide research, no cure has yet been devised. Though several drugs help slow its progress, so far AIDS has proved to be universally fatal.

Widespread malnutrition makes children especially vulnerable to disease.

School attendance is highest in the cities, where many children attend private institutions like this Roman Catholic school.

Education in Haiti, like health care, is far below world standards. Only 35 to 40 percent of the nation's adults can read and write, and many of these can read only a few simple words and write nothing but their own names. The school system for Haiti's poor black majority is especially inadequate. Education is free, but students must pay for their books, an intolerable burden for many families. Classes are often taught in French, which few Haitian children understand.

Children aged 6 through 12 are required by law to attend school, but in reality only about 25 percent finish primary school, and only about 15 percent go on to secondary school (high school). School attendance rates are highest among the children of the mulatto elite and the urban black middle class. These youngsters often attend private or parochial (Catholic) schools. The nation has only one college, the University of Haiti, founded in Port-au-Prince in 1944.

The annual carnival, or Mardi Gras, is a time of festivity, costumes, and parades.

Cultural Life

Haitian culture has traditionally mirrored the split in society between the French-inspired mulattoes and the African-inspired blacks. The elegant boulevards and imposing marble-and-wrought-iron buildings of Cap-Haïtien and Port-au-Prince reflect a French influence; the walled villages of the countryside and the busy, colorful street markets of the towns (including the two-block-long Iron Market in Port-au-Prince) are African in flavor. Mulatto girls and women study classical piano; the countryside moves to the beat of drummers and workers singing in the fields.

In recent years, however, Haitian literature and art have shown greater unity between the country's two cultures. As early as 1901, the French-influenced author Georges Sylvain wrote a collection of local fables in Creole and called it *Cric-crac*. (In Haitian tradition, a storyteller begins by asking, "Cric?" When a listener responds, "Crac!" the story begins.) During the 1920s, other French-oriented Haitian authors became interested in Creole folklore and culture. Author Jacques Romain's tales of peasant life became world famous; the best known is *Gouverneurs de la rosée* (Masters of the Dew). Today, many Haitian writers live abroad; during the reign of the Duvaliers, they moved to foreign countries where they could publish their work without fear of the censorship that marked the regimes of Papa Doc and his son.

Creole and folk traditions have also influenced modern composers and performers of music. Along with drums of all shapes and sizes, traditional Haitian music uses bamboo flutes, tambourines, marimbas, and horns made of conch shells. The Folklore Troupe of Haiti has carried this music—and the vigorous dances that accompany it—to audiences around the world. Jean Léon Destiné, a Haitian dancer who performed traditional dances to folk music, was popular in the United States and Europe in the 1960s and 1970s.

Haiti's rural life is filled with music. Nearly everyone can play some instrument; in addition, bands of three or more musicians often travel from village to village, entertaining residents in exchange for food and a place to sleep. Such occasions as weddings, birthdays, and funerals are frequently celebrated with a *bamboche*

Costumed carnival dancers practice a routine. The Folklore Troupe of Haiti has carried the country's traditional dances and music to audiences around the world.

(spree), an event that features music, dancing, food, drink, story-telling, and card games. The songs performed at these bamboches, as well as those sung to enliven the work of a combite, usually deal with local gossip, politics, scandal, history, and legend. Students of Haitian folklore have been making records of this lively music since the 1930s.

Painting is probably the best known of Haiti's art forms. Visiting Haiti in the 1940s, a number of American art collectors were struck by the vivid colors and original designs they saw on painted signs and doors in the countryside. The collectors provided painting materials, encouraged promising artists to express themselves, and helped to find buyers for the finished pictures. The result was the "Haitian Renaissance," an explosion of artistic production by untrained but talented painters. Characterized by bold shapes and colors, the work of these artists often depicts subjects drawn from religion or everyday life. Like the work of Grandma Moses in the United States, this popular school of Haitian art is described as "primitive" or "naive."

Haiti's most celebrated painters include Hector Hippolyte, Philomé Obin, Wilson Bigaud, and Castera Bazile. Obin, Bigaud, and Bazile were among the many artists who joined forces to decorate the Protestant Episcopal Cathedral of Ste. Trinité in Port-au-Prince in the late 1960s. Many of their cathedral murals use scenes from Haitian life to illustrate stories from the Bible. Obin, for example, showed Calvary (the hill where Christ was crucified) as a city street in Haiti. Bigaud's version of the wedding feast at Cana (the site, according to the New Testament, of Christ's first miracle) shows guests seated in Haitian-style rocking chairs and, in one corner of the picture, a Haitian policeman chasing a thief. Another striking work displayed in the cathedral is a dazzling construction of open-work ceramic blocks by sculptor Jasmin Joseph; it forms the screen behind which the choir is located.

Saints, Spirits, and Voodoo

Religion plays an extremely important role in Haitian life. And, just as Haiti has an official language, French, and a widespread popular language, Creole, it has an official religion and a popular one.

Roman Catholicism, Haiti's official religion, is the faith of about 80 percent of the population. Except for the mulatto elite and the well-educated urban blacks, however, almost all Haitians also practice Voodoo, a traditional folk religion. Uninformed people often think of Voodoo as a cult of black magic whose priests turn people into zombies and stick pins into the images of their enemies. But Voodoo is a genuine religion, involving communication with powers greater than humankind and unity with the forces of nature.

The Catholic church disapproves of Voodoo, but Voodoo believers see no conflict in practicing both religions at the same time. As poet Frank Fouche puts it: "We love the church, but we adore Voodoo." In fact, Christianity and Voodoo share a number of similar elements. Voodoo acknowledges the existence of a single creator of heaven and earth, the *Gran Mèt*, who delegates an array of powerful spirits called *loas* to deal with human life. Based on traditional Af-

A Christian woman carries a rock, a symbol of Jesus' carrying the cross.

Almost all Haitians practice Voodoo, a traditional folk religion.

rican spirits, loas are identified with Christian saints as well. Erzulie, the spirit of love, also represents the Virgin Mary; the African war god, Ougou Ferey, represents St. James; Papa Legba, patron of travelers, represents St. Peter.

The two faiths also share several important religious holidays. The largest and most famous celebration of these special days takes place every summer at Saut d'Eau, a waterfall near the mountain village of Ville Bonheur in central Haiti. The event commemorates a vision of the Virgin Mary that appeared to a local farmer at the waterfall. Each year, thousands of Haitians travel to Saut d'Eau to attend both the Catholic masses honoring the vision and the ceremonies honoring Erzulie and other Voodoo spirits.

Like many African religions, Voodoo is based on the concept of a life spirit that inhabits everything—people, trees, oceans, even the earth itself. The object of a Voodoo ceremony is to achieve communication with that universal spirit. A regular Voodoo worship service is conducted in a *hounfor* (temple), often a simple, whitewashed room with pictures of Catholic saints on the walls and mystical designs drawn in colored sand on the floor. Led by a *houngan* (male priest) or *mambo* (female priest) the service includes hours of drumming, dancing, and chanting.

When a participant feels that he or she has become possessed by a loa, that person has reached the goal of the service: communication with the universal spirit of life. At this point, the worshiper may fall into a hypnotic trance, losing his or her own personality and displaying the characteristics of the loa in possession. Individuals who become thus possessed are treated with great respect by their fellow believers: They have achieved union with the universe.

Voodoo also has a dark side. Among its practitioners are *bokors*, "sorcerers" who claim to be able to harness the power of the spirit world for evil purposes. Believed to be capable of casting spells that bring illness or bad luck, bokors are sometimes hired by people who wish to harm their rivals in love or business. Some anthropologists (scientists who study human societies) believe that the bokors use secret formulas of plant and animal poisons, perhaps dating from the days of the African slave trade, to bring about results. Stories of Haiti's legendary zombies, the "living dead" of horror movies, are probably based on the fact that certain bokor potions can make a person seem to die, only to be revived later by another potion.

Voodoo affects every part of Haitian daily life, especially in rural areas. Houngans and mambos are treated with deference, and their opinions are sought on such matters as matchmaking, arguments over property, and illness; many are skilled at preparing effective folk remedies. For the most part, Voodoo gives the people of Haiti the things that people everywhere seek in religion: an explanation of the world around them, a code of conduct, and a means of contacting the spirit world.

About 16 percent of Haiti's people belong to a third religious group, the Protestants; 10 percent are Baptists; the rest belong to an assortment of denominations. Protestantism, the newest faith to arrive in Haiti, is most popular among urban blacks. Many Protestant clergymen combine preaching with teaching, political protest, or aid programs, activities that have made them popular among many Haitians. Protestant Haitians are less likely than Catholics to be Voodooists, probably because Protestant symbols have not been incorporated into Voodoo belief as Catholic symbols have. In addition, many Protestants are well-educated city dwellers who wish to free themselves of peasant traditions and behavior. Some of these people believe that Voodoo has helped keep Haiti in a state of ignorance and political oppression.

President Préval inspects an irrigation canal. Under economic reform, proceeds from the sale of government-owned enterprises are used to finance development projects.

Haiti in Review

Perhaps the word that best describes modern Haiti—indeed, Haiti throughout much of its history—is "desperate." As the Western Hemisphere's most impoverished and overpopulated nation, it has endured almost unrelenting hardships. In health care, sanitation, education, housing, road building, and public-welfare programs, Haiti's resources lag far behind the needs of its people. This remains true despite modest gains in recent years.

Agriculture is the country's main economic activity, but soil erosion, overcrowding, and inefficient farming methods have made the soil continually less productive. Programs to reforest the hills, to introduce new crops and farming techniques, and to fertilize the exhausted soil have so far made only limited progress. Industry, still in its infancy, was dealt a serious blow by the economic sanctions levied by the United Nations against the country's illegitimate government; recovery, though underway, will be modest for some years to come. Tourism, which many Haitians had hoped would bring new life to their economy, was dealt the double blow of the AIDS crisis and a decade of violent political upheaval.

There are signs of hope. Following the restoration of democratic government, international aid has poured into Haiti, including hundreds of millions of dollars in grants and loans, volunteers from dozens of countries, and the expertise of professionals in health, educational, and economic matters. The elected government, for the first time, has given priority both to putting the country on a firm financial basis and to aiding, rather than exploiting, the poor majority. With the help of churches and labor groups, Haitians are now demanding a voice in shaping their own political future.

Haiti has seen many changes over the years. Site of the first European colony in America, it became a neglected Spanish outpost, then a pirate stronghold. In the 18th century it was the wealthiest French colony in the world. In the 19th century, it became the world's first black republic, a nation of freed slaves struggling, often in vain, to establish an independent and stable government. Then, in the 20th century, Haiti spent two decades under occupation by the United States, three decades under a family dictatorship, and almost two more under a succession of brutal, rapacious military rulers.

Today, Haiti remains a land where a majority of its citizens live at a bare subsistence level, and many die of disease and malnutrition. Yet, with a democratic constitution and a young but concerned administration, Haiti has found some sense of hope; the worst may be past. Entering the 21st century, Haiti's future looks somewhat brighter.

◄GLOSSARY►

affranchi   Literally, "freeman." A term used during the colonial period to describe free mulattoes.

bokor   A Voodoo sorceror, believed to possess the powers of black magic.

boucan   A framework of green wood on which meat is smoked. The 17th-century pirates who practiced this came to be known as "buccaneers."

cacique   An Arawak chieftain or head of a village.

caco   A mercenary or soldier of fortune.

combite   An informal work group of rural neighbors who help each other with tasks such as clearing fields or building houses in return for parties and entertainment.

Creole   The language of the black population; Haiti's unofficial language. Creole combines French words, as well as a few Spanish and African words, with African pronunciations and sentence structure.

gens de couleur   Literally, "people of color." Used to describe free mulattoes during the colonial period.

gourde   Haiti's national currency, divided into 100 centimes. A gourde is worth about U.S. $.20.

gros habitant   A rural term for a person of some wealth, power, or local standing; a "big shot."

gros neg   Literally, "big nose." See *gros habitant.*

hounfor   A Voodoo temple, often the priest's house.

houngan A Voodoo priest.

junta A ruling committee or council, usually composed of military officers.

loa A Voodoo god or spirit, usually combining the characteristics of a traditional African deity with those of a Christian figure.

mambo A voodoo priestess.

maroon The term applied to runaway slaves throughout the Caribbean region during the colonial period. In Haiti, the maroon communities led the slave revolt.

mulatto A person of mixed black and white ancestry.

plaçage A system of common-law marriage common in Haiti. Under plaçage, men are allowed to have more than one mate and family, and it is socially acceptable for both men and women to have more than one sexual partner.

repartimiento A plan of land allotment designed by Christopher Columbus and used widely in Spanish colonies throughout Central and South America. The repartimiento system gave large land grants and everything on them, including the Indians, to Spanish colonists.

Tonton Macoutes Literally, "Uncle Knapsack." The term refers to ogres or evil men who, in Haitian folklore, kidnap children in sacks. Tontons Macoutes is the name given to the secret police and terrorist force created by François Duvalier.

Voodoo A religion native to Haiti that combines traditional West African belief in spirits and magic with the saints and rituals of the Roman Catholic Church. Voodoo includes a complex code of social behavior and profoundly influences the daily lives of most Haitian peasants.

◄ I N D E X ►

A

AIDS, 23, 92
Arawak, 27, 39, 40, 43, 53
Aristide, Jean-Bertand, 21, 23, 35, 74–75
Artibonite River, 31, 32
Avril, Prosper, 73, 75

B

Bamboche, 96
Baron Samedi, 70
Bazile, Castera, 97
Bennett, Michèle, 71
Bigaud, Wilson, 97
Bokors, 100
Boucans, 43
Boukman, 49, 50
Bourgs, 78
Boyer, Jean-Pierre, 56

C

Cacos, 65–67
Cailles, 91
Cap-Français, 44
Cap-Haïtien, 29, 40, 49, 54, 65, 72, 78, 83, 95
Chaîne de Matheux, 28, 29
Christophe, Henri, 50, 52–56
Ciboney, 39
Citadelle La Ferrière, 24, 55
Cité Soleil, 88
Clairin, 91

Columbus, Christopher, 23, 25, 40–42
Combite, 90, 97
Communes, 78
Cortés, Hernando, 42
Court of Cassation, 78
Creole, 24, 85–87, 95, 96, 98
Cric-crac (Sylvain), 95
Cuba, 17, 27
Cul-de-Sac, 29

D

Deforestation, 34, 35
Départements, 78
Dessalines, Jean-Jacques, 50, 52, 53, 56
Destiné, Jean Léon, 96
D'Ogeron, Bertrand, 44
Dominican Republic, 17, 20, 27–29, 32–34, 40, 42, 56, 67, 68, 75
Duvalier, François ("Papa Doc"), 21, 23, 69–71, 77, 95
Duvalier, Jean-Claude ("Baby Doc"), 21, 23, 70–72, 77, 95
Dysentery, 23, 92

E

Erzulie, 99
Estimé, Dumarsais, 68, 69
Étang Saumâtre, 32, 37

F

Ferdinand, king of Spain, 40
Folklore Troupe of Haiti, 96
Fort-Liberté, 78
Fouche, Frank, 98
France, 44–46, 49, 52, 65, 72
French Revolution, 47, 49

G

Geffrard, Nicholas-Fabre, 65
Gonaïves, 78, 83
Gourde, 81
Gouverneurs de la rosée (Romain),
    95
Grande Anse, 32
Grande Cayemite, 30, 31
Gran Mèt, 98
Gros habitants, 89
Gros negs, 89
Gulf of Gonâve, 27, 29–31

H

Haiti
    agriculture in, 18, 79, 80, 90,
        103
    armed forces of, 78, 79
    art of, 97
    constitution of, 73–74, 77
    culture of, 95–101
    dress in, 87, 88, 91
    economy of, 79–82, 103
    education in, 93, 103
    fishing industry in, 81
    food in, 87, 91
    foreign aid to, 103, 104
    French rule of, 19, 44–47,
        104. *See also* Saint-
        Domingue
    geography of, 27
    health system of, 91–92, 103
    industry in, 18, 81, 103
    judicial system of, 78
    music of, 96, 97
    natural resources in, 79
    population of, 17
    public-health problems of, 22,
        23, 92, 103
    religion in, 98–101
    slave rebellion in, 49–51, 53
    slums in, 88
    Spanish rule of, 40–44, 104
    transportation in, 82, 83
    voting rights in, 77
Haitian Renaissance, 97
Hinche, 78
Hippolyte, Hector, 97
Hispaniola, 17, 21, 25, 27, 32, 34,
    40–44, 51, 56
Hounfor, 99
Houngan, 99, 100
Hurricanes, 33
Hyppolite, Florvil, 65

I

Ile à Vache, 30
Isabella, queen of Spain, 40

J

Jacmel, 78, 83
Jamaica, 17
James, C. L. R., 50
Jeremie, 78
Joseph, Jasmin, 97

L

La Gonâve, 27, 29
Lake Miragoâne, 32, 37
Lake Péligre, 32

Lambi Island, 31
La Navidad, 23, 41
Lavalas party, 75
Leclerc, Charles, 52
Les Cayes, 78
Lescot, Élie, 68
Loas, 98, 100
Louis XIV, king of France, 44

M

Magloire, Paul, 68, 69
Malaria, 23, 37, 92
Malnutrition, 23, 92
Mambo, 99, 100
Manigat, Leslie, 73
Maroons, 50
Massacre River, 32
Massif de la Selle, 28, 35
Massif du Nord, 28, 29, 31
Massif du Sud, 28
Montagnes Noires, 28, 29
Morison, Samuel Eliot, 42
Mulattoes, 17, 20, 46, 47, 49–53, 56,
    68, 85, 87, 93, 95, 98

N

Namphy, Henri, 73
Napoléon Bonaparte, 52, 55
National Assembly, 73

O

Obin, Philomé, 97
Ogé, Jacques Vincent, 49
Ougou Ferey, 99

P

Papa Legba, 99
Paul VI, 70

Pedernales River, 32
Péligre Dam, 32
Pétion, Alexandre Sabès, 54, 56
Pic la Selle, 28
Pirates, 30, 43, 104
Pizarro, Francisco, 43
Plaçage, 91
Plaine Centrale, 29
Plaine de l'Artibonite, 29, 31, 32, 35,
    45, 91
Plaine du Nord, 29, 45
Port-au-Prince, 29, 30, 32, 33, 65,
    78, 83, 85–88, 91, 93, 95, 97
Port-de-Paix, 30, 32, 44
Préval, René, 75
Protestant Episcopal Cathedral of
    Ste. Trinité, 97

R

Repartimiento, 42
Romain, Jacques, 95
Roman Catholic church, 65, 70, 98

S

Saint-Domingue, 19, 20, 44–47, 49,
    51, 52
Sam, Vilbrun Guillaume, 65, 66
Sans Souci, 54, 55
Santo Domingo, 42, 43, 51, 52, 56
Saut d'Eau, 99
Slaves, 17, 19, 20, 42, 44–47, 49–51,
    104
Soulouque, Faustin-Élie, 56
Spain, 42, 43, 44, 51, 54
Sugarcane, 19, 22, 45, 80
Sylvain, Georges, 95

T

Taino, 40–42

Tap-taps, 82
Tontons Macoutes, 69–74, 79
Tortuga, 30, 43
Tourism, 22, 23, 82, 103
Toussaint L'Ouverture, François-Dominique, 50–53
Treaty of Ryswick, 44
Trois Rivières, 31
Tuberculosis, 23, 92

U
University of Haiti, 93

V
Vincent, Sténio, 67, 68
Voodoo, 24, 70, 72, 85, 98–101

W
West Indies, 17, 40
Windward Passage, 27, 66
World War I, 66

PICTURE CREDITS

AP/Wide World Photos: pp. 24, 38, 54, 73, 74, 76, 83, 87, 98, 102; The Bettmann Archive: pp. 2, 19, 21, 28, 30, 41, 44, 45, 48, 50, 55, 88; Chip Chamberlain: p. 63; Culver Pictures: pp. 53, 66, 67; Eric Kroll/Taurus Photos: pp. 58, 60–61; Jason Lauré: p. 70; Library of Congress: pp. 31, 36, 86, 92, 93; Organization of American States: pp. 16, 96; Reuters/Bettmann Newsphotos: pp. 78, 79; Donna Sinisgalli: pp. 6–7; Claire Taplin/Taurus Photos: pp. 26, 57, 58–59, 59, 62 (below); United Nations: pp. 18, 22, 60 (above), 61, 62 (above), 64, 84; UPI/Bettmann Newsphotos: pp. 33, 68, 69, 71, 72, 80, 82, 89, 94, 99